ANIMAL STORY

CITY BEAR

by Dougal Dixon

WATERBIRD BOOKS

Columbus, Ohio

ANIMAL STORY

CITY BEAR

Children's Publishing

This edition published in the United States of America in 2004 by
Waterbird Books
an imprint of McGraw-Hill Children's Publishing,
a Division of The McGraw-Hill Companies
8787 Orion Place
Columbus, Ohio 43240-4027

www.MHkids.com

Library of Congress Cataloging-in-Publication Data is on file with the publisher.

First published in Great Britain in 2004 by *ticktock* Media Ltd.,
Unit 2 Orchard Business Centre, North Farm Road, Tunbridge Wells, Kent TN3 3XF.
Text and illustrations © 2004 *ticktock* Entertainment Ltd.
We would like to thank: Downs Matthews, Director Emeritus, Polar Bears International, Jean Coppendale and Elizabeth Wiggans.
Every effort has been made to trace the copyright holders, and we apologize in advance for any unintentional omissions.
We would be pleased to insert the appropriate acknowledgements in any subsequent edition of this publication.

Printed in China

1-57768-880-5

1 2 3 4 5 6 7 8 9 10 TTM 09 08 07 06 05 04

The McGraw·Hill Companies

CONTENTS

THALIE THE POLAR BEAR IS BORN

Thalie's world is a safe, warm, white cave, about the size of a desk—3 feet high and 6 feet long. She shares this den with her mother and her twin brother, Mari.

The family is separated from the winter darkness and biting cold by 6 feet of snow, with only a narrow breathing hole leading to the outside world.

Thalie is four weeks old, and her eyes have just opened for the first time. It will be another two or three weeks before she is able to stand up and walk around in the den. She is growing fast, though, feeding on her mother's milk.

When Thalie and Mari were born, they each weighed only one pound, which is as much as a jar of peanut butter. Their mother weighs close to 600 pounds, which is as much as three or four men. She is the biggest land-living predator on earth.

It is early April. Thalie and Mari are now three months old, and it is time for the family to leave the den.

First, their mother digs through the snow that blocks the den's entrance tunnel. Then, she sniffs the air for signs of other animals, such as wolves or male polar bears, that may kill the cubs for food. When she is sure that they are safe, she leads the cubs into the bright, spring day.

The bears live in the Arctic Circle, which is the region at the top of the earth. Icy land surrounds the Arctic Ocean, where a large area of the sea is permanently frozen. This frozen area is known as the "ice cap." In winter, the ice cap expands and pushes up against the edges of the land.

During the short Arctic summer, some of the ice on land thaws, and plants begin to grow. Throughout the long Arctic winter, the ground is bare, and most life is found in the sea.

The cold waters are home to squid, fish, whales, and seals. In some places, the changing currents break up the sea ice. This is ideal for the seals because they need to leave the water from time to time. The frozen ice also helps the polar bears. When the seals leave the water, the bears can hunt them on the sea ice.

TIME TO GO OUTSIDE

With their little eyes blinking, Thalie and Mari scramble from the warmth of the den into the fresh, spring air.

Their mother is right at home in the Arctic. Her huge body is designed to survive in this cold environment. She has two layers of fur: an outer layer of oily guard hairs and a short, woolly undercoat. Her fur looks white, but each strand is actually transparent. The see-through hairs have a hollow core that scatters and reflects light, making the fur look white. Beneath her fur, she has black skin that absorbs heat and a thick layer of fat, called *blubber*, that stops the heat from escaping.

Polar bears can get too hot. An overheated polar bear will cool off by gulping a mouthful of snow, swimming, or lying flat on the cold ground. Polar bears spend much of their lives in the sea. They use their big, broad feet as paddles when they swim. When they are out of the water, polar bears walk on ice. A covering of fine hair on the soles of their feet keeps the bears from slipping on the ice.

Thalie and Mari's first venture into the open air is a short one, and they soon return to the den. Their mother has had nothing to eat for five or six months and she is ready to hunt. But the family will not travel far from this spot for at least another two weeks.

Polar bears are strong swimmers.
Today, Thalie and Mari are going to learn this
important skill. The cubs follow their mother from the den,
across the snow and ice, toward the water's edge.

Their mother plunges into the icy waves, but Thalie and Mari do not make the quick plunge. This is the first time they have seen the sea. The mother bear slips through the icy water. She paddles with her webbed front feet and uses her hind feet to steer her body. Her streamlined body hardly leaves a ripple in the water.

Mari jumps in, and Thalie follows. The cubs kick and splutter, but they quickly learn how to move through the water. Swimming is hard work. Soon, the babies climb onto their mother's back. The family swims to the shore. Thalie and Mari's first swimming lesson has been a success.

ARCTIC LIFE

Human beings influence all regions of the earth.

In the last hundred years, mining and drilling companies have gone to the Arctic looking for oil, gas, valuable metals, and diamonds beneath the frozen surface. The mess and pollution that are left behind can harm the polar bears and their food sources.

At one time, many hunters came to the Arctic to hunt and kill polar bears. By the 1970s, hunters had killed so many polar bears that activists felt something had to be done. In 1976, laws were passed limiting the number of bears that hunters could kill. In some cases, the laws banned hunting completely.

The native people who live close to the territory of Thalie and her family are the Inuit. These people have lived here for hundreds of years, netting fish, harpooning seals, and hunting polar bears. The Inuit are still allowed to hunt the bears in some places, but they are strictly limited to a specific number each year.

Now, visitors come to watch the bears. Special buses with all-weather tires roll across the ice while tourists take photographs of the animals from the safety of the vehicles.

A year has passed since the cubs were born. Thalie and Mari have been eating seal meat since they were four months old, but they still drink their mother's rich, fatty milk.

It is spring again, and the cubs are learning to hunt ringed seals for themselves. This is a good time of year to hunt seals. The young seal pups in a nearby colony are inexperienced and cannot swim. They are stranded on the ice. Thalie's mother leaves her two youngsters behind and slips silently into the water, heading toward the seals. It is not just the seal pups that are inexperienced, though.

Thalie and Mari are watching their mother, and they do not notice the band of Inuit creeping up behind them with their ropes and harpoons.

Suddenly, the hunters attack! The startled cubs dive into the water, calling for their mother. Thalie scrambles ashore to safety. Her mother swims to meet her, and the two females look back. Mari is trapped, caught by the hunters' ropes and surrounded by dogs. There is nothing Thalie and her mother can do to help him. They will never see Mari again.

THALIE, THE ADULT POLAR BEAR

Thalie is now four years old and has left her mother. Last spring, a male bear began to follow the pair of females. Thalie's mother was ready to breed again, and her mother's new mate chased Thalie away.

Now, Thalie roams the floating ice cap, hunting for herself. She commonly visits certain hunting sites across several hundred square miles. Thalie's white fur helps to blend in with the ice and snow. Then, she is able to creep up on colonies of beached seals and their pups. She has also learned to find the holes in the ice that the adult seals use to come up for air.

Thalie will wait beside a seal
airhole for up to four hours. At just the right moment, she leaps. Her great weight
crashes through the ice. Thalie drags the seal out of the water and kills it with a single
blow from her huge paw. She quickly eats the rich, fatty blubber, while a pack of
Arctic foxes watch her and wait for her leftovers.

Thalie smells something in the air. Rotting meat—food! She follows the scent for many miles along the shoreline and finally comes to the source. A dead bowhead whale has washed up on the ice.

But, Thalie is not alone. Polar bears have the best sense of smell in the animal kingdom, and many other bears have also arrived at the scene, attracted by the smell of the carcass.

Thalie moves in to join the others. They do not fight because there is plenty of meat for everyone. This will probably be their last big meal of the spring. Summer is coming. Soon, the sea ice will begin to melt and break up, making it difficult for the polar bears to hunt for seals among the broken pieces.

Thalie and the other bears will wander inland onto the tundra. Here, the topsoil thaws during the summer while the ground underneath stays permanently frozen. The bears can search for food on the swampy ground. Thalie will eat grass, small plants, and berries. The only meat she will find will be small rodents, such as lemmings and nesting birds.

Polar bears are adaptable animals, though. As well as being a hunter, Thalie can be a scavenger. When meat is scarce, Thalie can even survive on only vegetation.

Summer is over, and the floating
ice is building up along the shore again.
With the ice come the seals. Thalie and the
other bears begin to move northward once more.

Thalie is pregnant. While she was scavenging the whale carcass, she met and mated with a big male bear. Like most pregnant polar bears, Thalie will probably give birth to twin cubs. Her pregnancy will last about eight months. Once winter is underway, Thalie will dig a den where she can give birth in January. Her baby or babies will not grow for the first months of her pregnancy. For now, Thalie will need to hunt as much meat as possible. Her fat reserves need to last her through the winter. As she ventures northward, her long, sensitive nose smells something strange. It is a town with houses, garbage dumps, and restaurants.

POLAR BEAR IN THE CITY

Hungry and curious, Thalie lumbers along the main street of the town. Dogs bark and people hurry inside!

A polar bear wandering through the town is not a new situation for the people in this region, though. It happens every year, so there is a system in place to deal with the situation. The size and strength of polar bears make them very dangerous animals. A team of specially-trained hunters is summoned. They are called a *Polar Bear Alert Team*.

As Thalie investigates the town dump, the team creeps up on her. If the team disturbs her, she may panic and cause damage. If the team angers her, she may attack in self-defense. The leader of the team loads his rifle and finds himself a good place from which to shoot. Thalie is unaware of the danger. The man raises his rifle and shoots!

But it is not a bullet that he fires. It is an anesthetic dart that will cause Thalie to fall asleep. The people of the town do not want the polar bears to harm them, but they also do not want to kill the polar bears. Within a few moments, she becomes sleepy. Then, she collapses in the street!

Thalie wakes. She is lying by the sea. Out at sea, there are drifting ice floes, and the water is full of seals—food!

While Thalie was unconscious, she was bundled up in a net and lifted from the main street of the town by a helicopter. Her body was carried, dangling and swinging, away to the north and far from people and their towns.

Every year, many bears are moved to safety in this way. Sometimes, while the bears are

unconscious, they are fitted with radio collars. The collars send signals, through satellite, to a receiving station. There, scientists can track the bears to find out where they travel.

The team waits for Thalie to regain consciousness. When they are sure that she is okay, they prepare to leave.

The whirring, rattling helicopter rises, but Thalie does not seem to notice. She is busy hunting for food.

A NEW BEGINNING

Thalie's world is a safe, warm, white cave, about the size of a desk—3 feet high and 6 feet long. Soon she will share this den with her own cub or cubs.

Thalie is preparing to hibernate. At the first heavy fall of snow, she finds a snowy slope on the north side of a hill. If the weather suddenly turns warmer, the snow on this slope will not melt. Then, she digs a tunnel and hollows out a chamber big enough to hold her and her litter.

Thalie's successful hunting helped her gain nearly 440 pounds in weight. Her coat has taken on a yellowish color from the body oils of the seals she has eaten. Thalie will need these fat reserves, because her baby or babies will start to grow inside her soon. Then, in January, as she sleeps, her cub or cubs will be born.

Polar bears no longer face extinction. This is a result of active conservation groups that protect the bears from overhunting and pollution. For now, the future for Thalie and her cubs is secure.

POLAR BEAR FACT FILE

The polar bear's scientific name is Ursus maritimus, ***meaning "bear of the sea."***
Polar bears used to be called *Thalarctos maritimus* ("ocean bear of the sea"). In the 1980s, genetic studies showed that the polar bear is so closely related to *Ursus arctos*, the brown bear (or grizzly bear), that it must be a species of *Ursus*. Polar bears are considered to be quite a new species. Scientists believe they evolved from brown bears only about 200,000 to 400,000 years ago.

THE WORLD OF THE POLAR BEAR

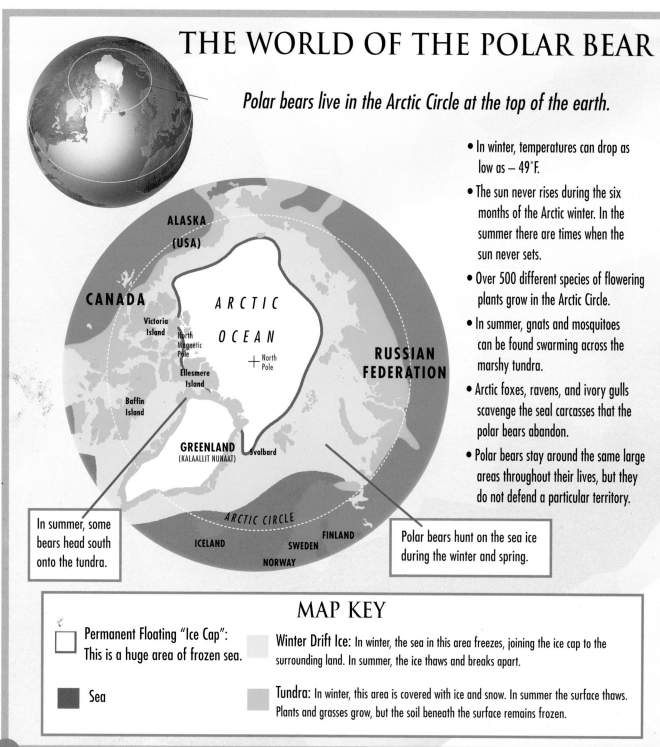

Polar bears live in the Arctic Circle at the top of the earth.

- In winter, temperatures can drop as low as − 49°F.

- The sun never rises during the six months of the Arctic winter. In the summer there are times when the sun never sets.

- Over 500 different species of flowering plants grow in the Arctic Circle.

- In summer, gnats and mosquitoes can be found swarming across the marshy tundra.

- Arctic foxes, ravens, and ivory gulls scavenge the seal carcasses that the polar bears abandon.

- Polar bears stay around the same large areas throughout their lives, but they do not defend a particular territory.

ALASKA (USA)

CANADA

ARCTIC OCEAN

Victoria Island

North Magnetic Pole

+ North Pole

RUSSIAN FEDERATION

Ellesmere Island

Baffin Island

GREENLAND (KALAALLIT NUNAAT)

Svalbard

ARCTIC CIRCLE

ICELAND

SWEDEN

FINLAND

NORWAY

In summer, some bears head south onto the tundra.

Polar bears hunt on the sea ice during the winter and spring.

MAP KEY

☐ **Permanent Floating "Ice Cap":** This is a huge area of frozen sea.

Winter Drift Ice: In winter, the sea in this area freezes, joining the ice cap to the surrounding land. In summer, the ice thaws and breaks apart.

■ **Sea**

Tundra: In winter, this area is covered with ice and snow. In summer the surface thaws. Plants and grasses grow, but the soil beneath the surface remains frozen.

PHYSICAL CHARACTERISTICS

The tail is 3½ – 4½ inches long

FEMALE

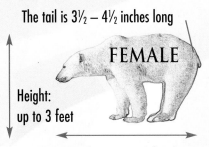

Height: up to 3 feet

Length: 5¾ – 6½ feet long
Weight: 440 – 770 pounds

MALE

Height: 4 feet or more

Length: 6½ – 9¾ feet long
Weight: 880 – 1,320 pounds

- Polar bears are the biggest land-living predators on earth.

- The polar bear has two layers of fur: an outer layer of oily guard hairs and a short, woolly undercoat.

- Polar bear fur looks white, but each strand is actually transparent. A hollow core in the hairs reflects light, making the fur look white.

- The polar bear's black skin absorbs heat.

- Polar bear blubber is approximately 4 inches thick.

- Polar bears have small ears and small noses. Small facial features keep them safe from frostbite!

- The polar bear has 42 teeth and a bluish-black tongue.

- Polar bear paws measure about 11½ inches across, or the size of a dinner plate! The paws are webbed for swimming and have hair on the soles to help the bears grip the ice.

- Only female bears can wear radio collars (see page 24). Male bears' necks are thicker than their heads, so the collars just fall off!

- The polar bear's body is streamlined for swimming.

ARCTIC FOOD WEB

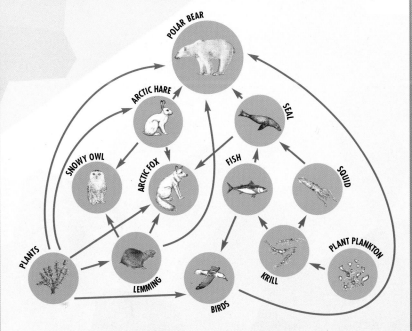

This food web shows how the animals and plants living in the Arctic Circle depend on each other for food—both on land and in the sea. The arrows in the web mean "give food to."

DIET

- The polar bear's main food is the ringed seal. They will also hunt harp seals and hooded seals.

- Polar bears will hunt and eat young walruses, beluga whales, narwhals, and dolphins.

- Fully-grown polar bears eat mainly the seal's rich, fatty blubber, leaving the red meat. This meat is scavenged by younger bears, who need the protein.

- When food is scarce, polar bears will eat lemmings, nesting birds and their eggs, berries— such as Arctic bilberries, cranberries, and raspberries—grass, moss, and lichens.

- Polar bears have even been seen eating seaweed!

CONSERVATION

- Polar bears are the only bears that are protected internationally.
- Scientists estimate that there are 25,000—40,000 polar bears in the world.
- In 1976, the US, Canada, Denmark, Russia, and Norway passed laws limiting the number of polar bears that hunters could kill. In some cases, the laws ban hunting completely. In some places, Inuit are still allowed to hunt a strictly agreed upon number of bears each year.

- Mining and drilling companies look for oil, gas, diamonds, and valuable metals beneath the frozen surface of the Arctic. Conservationists are monitoring the effects that any pollution (chemicals or oil spills for example) is having on the polar bears and their food sources.

BEHAVIOR AND SENSES

- Polar bears walk at about 3.4 mph. This slow, but steady, pace keeps them from overheating. If charging or fleeing, a polar bear can run at speeds of up to 25 mph, but for only a very short time.
- Polar bears are so well adapted to the cold, that they sometimes get too hot! They cool off by swimming, spreading their bellies on the icy ground, or by eating snow!
- Polar bears are strong swimmers. They can stay underwater for two minutes, and they have been known to swim up to 100 miles at a time.

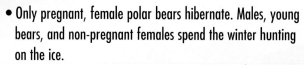

- Only pregnant, female polar bears hibernate. Males, young bears, and non-pregnant females spend the winter hunting on the ice.
- Polar bears have the best sense of smell in the animal kingdom. They can smell a potential meal from 20 miles away!

REPRODUCTION AND YOUNG

- The polar bear mating season is March to May.
- Pregnant female bears dig out a den on the north side of a slope or hill. They dig an entrance tunnel and a chamber where they spend the winter and give birth to their cub or cubs.

- Cubs are born from January to February.
- New cubs are known as COYS (Cubs of the Year—this year's cubs).
- When they are born, cubs are less than 12 inches long and weigh about 1 pound, or as much as a small bag of sugar.
- Cubs leave the den when they are about three months old. By this time, they are about 15 inches long and weigh about 28 pounds, or as much as a medium-sized dog.
- Mother bears wait until spring temperatures reach about 50°F before taking their cubs outside the den.
- Mother polar bears will carry the cubs on their backs if the babies get too tired.
- Cubs stay with their mother and continue to drink her rich, fatty milk for two to three years.
- Polar bears are attentive mothers. They groom and touch their cubs frequently.

GLOSSARY

ADAPTED When the bodies of a species of animal have changed to help them adjust to a new environment. Polar bear bodies have adapted to suit the cold temperatures in the Arctic.

ANESTHETIC A drug or gas used to put an animal or person to sleep. It is normally used during operations.

ARCTIC CIRCLE The area in the north that includes the Arctic Ocean and the northernmost parts of Asia, Europe, and North America. The area is shown on maps by an imaginary line.

BLUBBER Body fat that mammals (such as polar bears, seals, and whales) use for insulation and as a back-up energy source when food is limited.

CLIMATE The average temperature and weather conditions in a region over a period of years.

CONSERVATION GROUPS Organizations that look after the environment and campaign for the protection of wild animals. Their work can involve many different activities—campaigning against the hunting of endangered animals, cleaning up areas of land or sea that have been polluted, and talking to governments to try to pass laws that protect the environment.

HARPOON A type of spear with barbs (small points) at the end. Harpoons are sometimes attached to a rope.

HIBERNATE To sleep through the winter in a den or burrow to save energy.

ICE CAP The huge area of permanently frozen sea in the Arctic Ocean. The ice in the middle is about 32 feet thick.

ICE FLOE A sheet of floating ice.

LICHEN A plant-like partnership between a fungus and an algae. Lichen can grow on all sorts of bare surfaces, such as rocks or tree trunks.

INUIT The eskimo people who were born in and now live in Canada.

POLLUTION Oils, garbage, or chemicals that have escaped into the air or sea or onto the land. Pollution can damage the environment and harm wild animals and the food that they eat.

SCAVENGER An animal that eats other animals' leftovers or carrion (animals that are already dead).

STREAMLINED When something has a smooth shape and is able to move faster through air or water because there is less resistance.

TUNDRA A swampy landscape of low-growing plants. Below the surface, the ground is permanently frozen.

INDEX

PICTURE CREDITS

t=top, b=bottom, c=center, l=left, r=right, OFC=outside front cover, OBC=outside back cover

Alamy: OFC, 1c, 4-5, 6-7bc, 8tl, 9t, 10-11, 12-13t, 14-15, 16, 20-21, 22-23, 24-25c, 26-27, 30tl, 30b, OBC. Bryan & Cherry Alexander Photography: 13br. Corbis: 6-7 (background), 8-9b, 17, 18-19, 24lc, 24-25 (background), 30tr, 31.

Every effort has been made to trace the copyright holders, and we apologize in advance for any unintentional omissions. We would be pleased to insert the appropriate acknowledgements in any subsequent edition of this publication.